# ON THE ETHICS OF AESTHETICS

*Nathan Coppedge*

# ON THE ETHICS OF AESTHETICS

## BY NATHAN COPPEDGE

*Nathan Coppedge*

## INTRODUCTION

This writing comes
inspired in part by
Mr. Graberek's art
class.

*Nathan Coppedge*

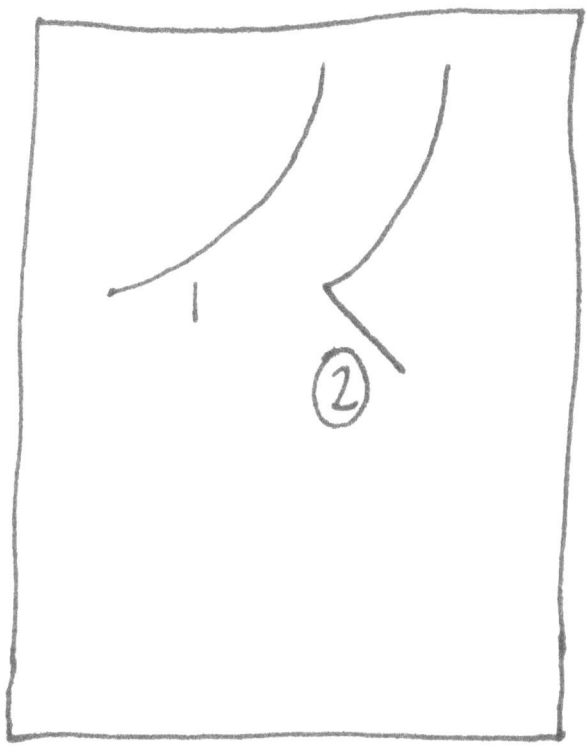

Sometimes an artistic choice is, upon circumspection, obvious.

*Nathan Coppedge*

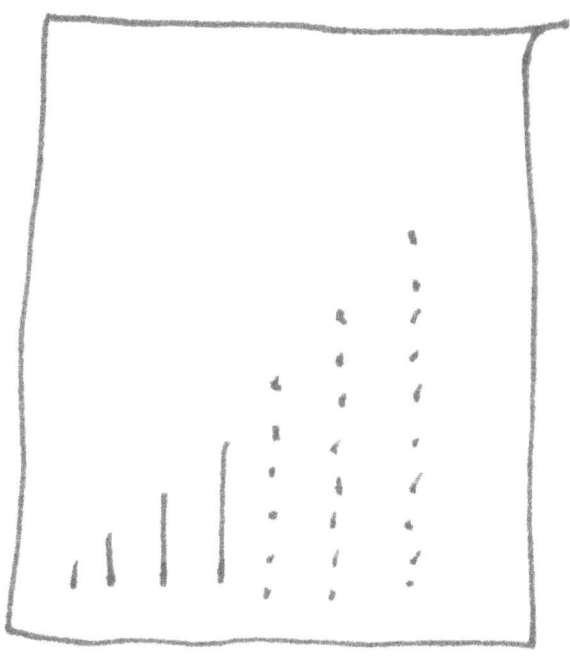

Regularity is sometimes good...

*Nathan Coppedge*

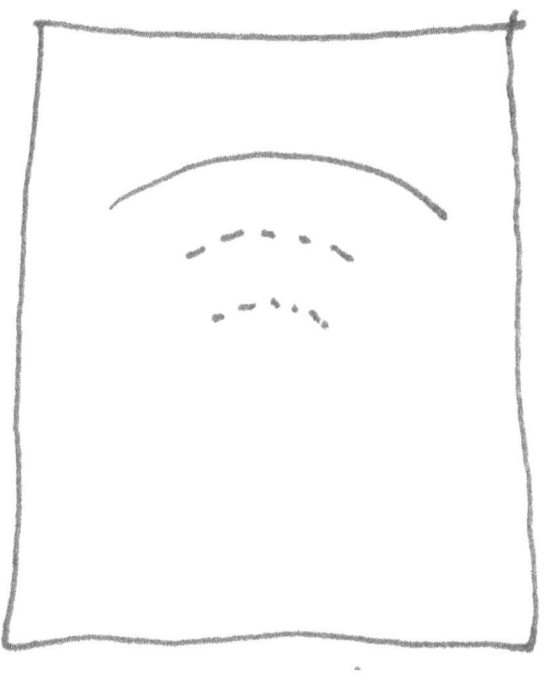

(Regularity).

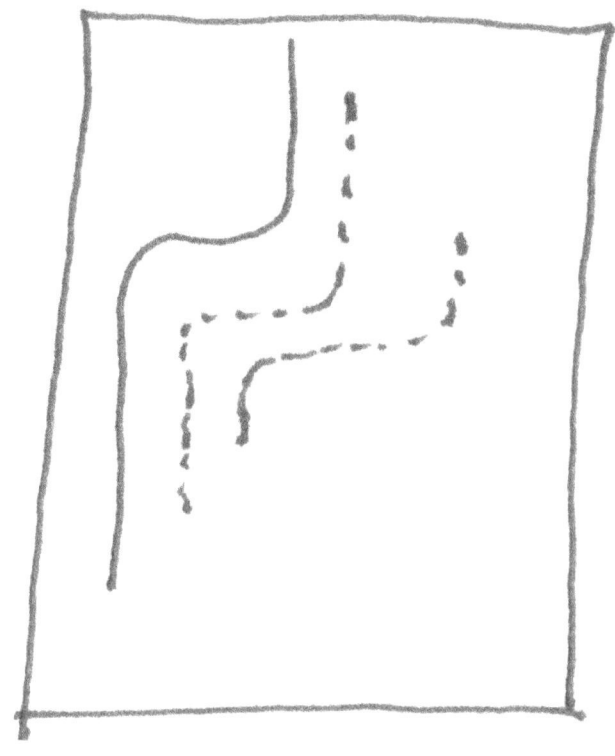

(Semi-regularity).

*Nathan Coppedge*

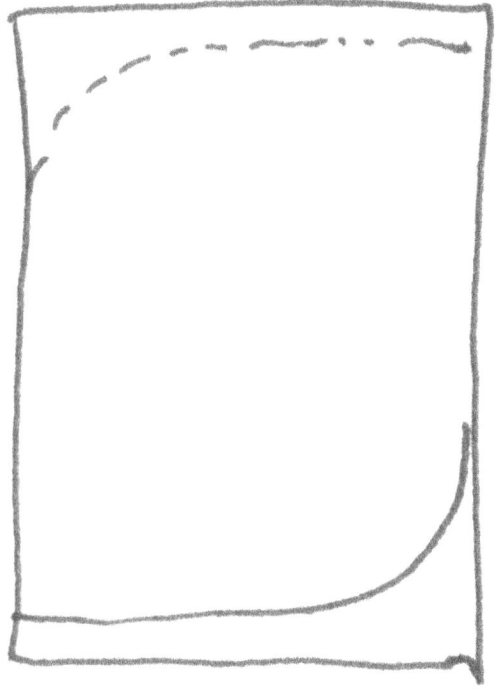

Desirable Symmetries...

*Nathan Coppedge*

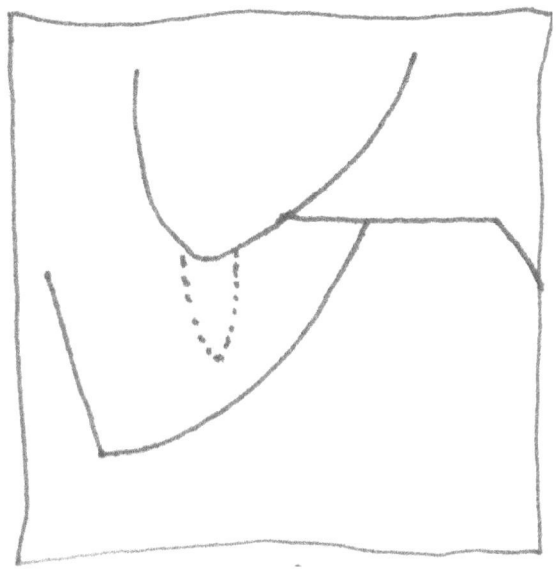

Rare 260-degree turn!

*Nathan Coppedge*

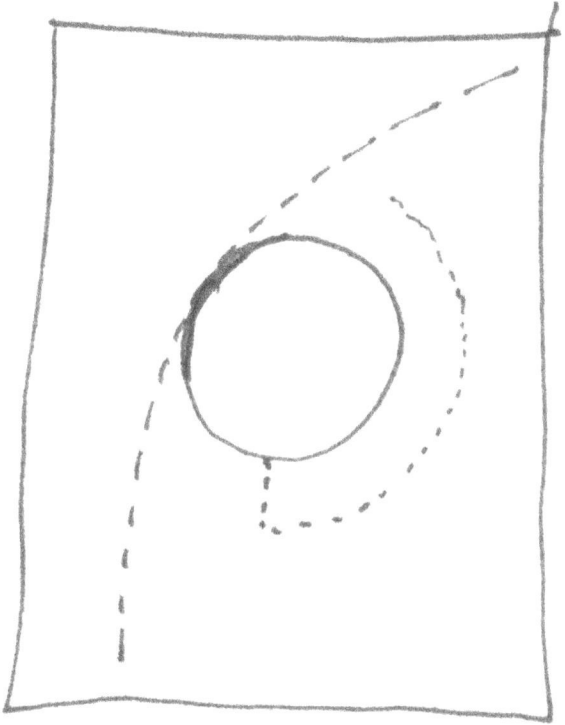

Options can be posed together, but not efficiently.

*Nathan Coppedge*

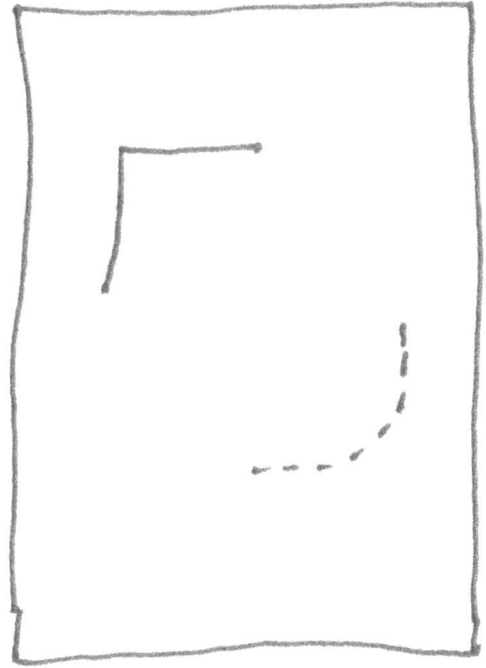

A clever form of variation.

*Nathan Coppedge*

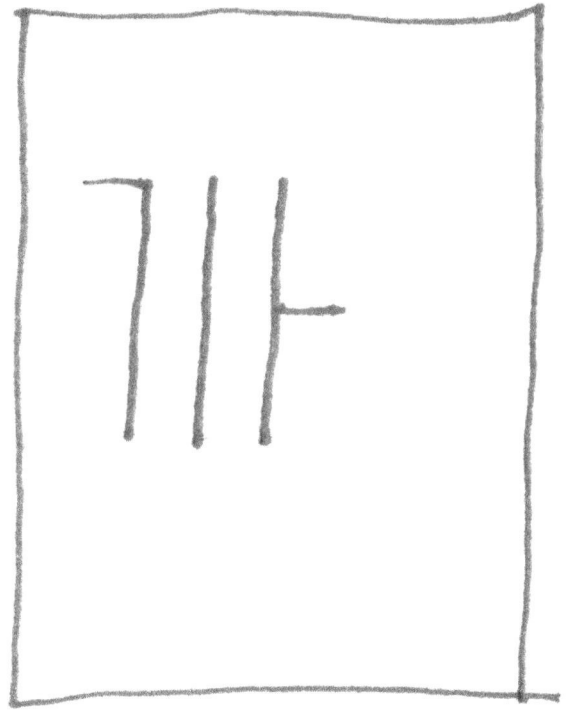

Orderly variation can be
juxtaposed with empty space.

*Nathan Coppedge*

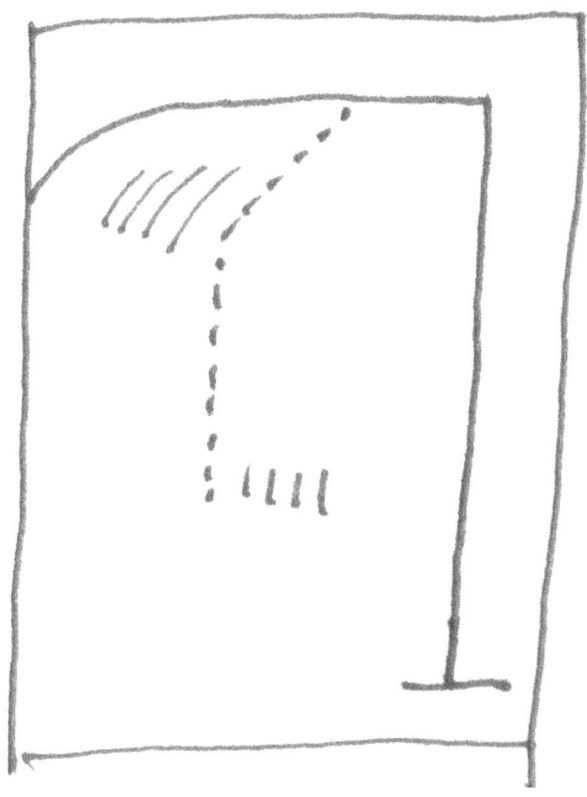

Initial work can be used to
  frame variations.

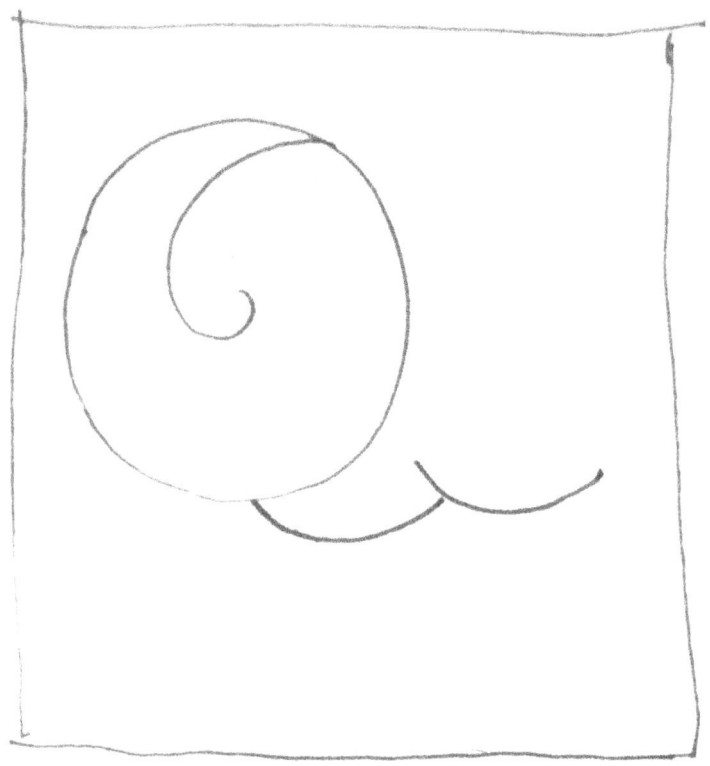

Circles imply spirals and nature.

*Nathan Coppedge*

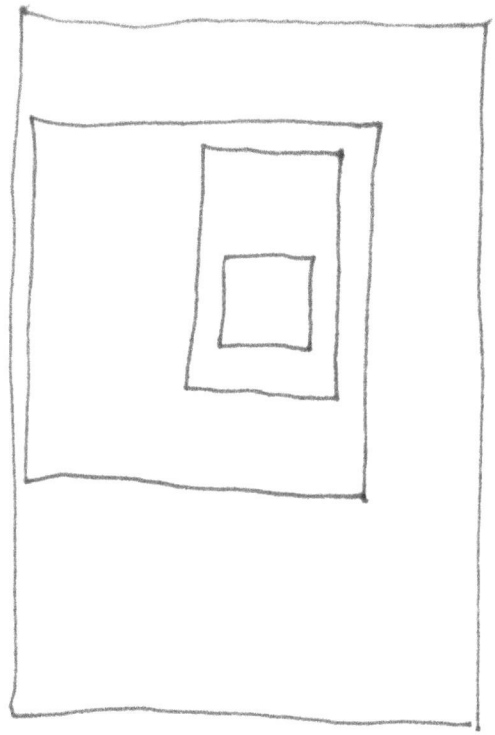

Squares imply rectangles.

*Nathan Coppedge*

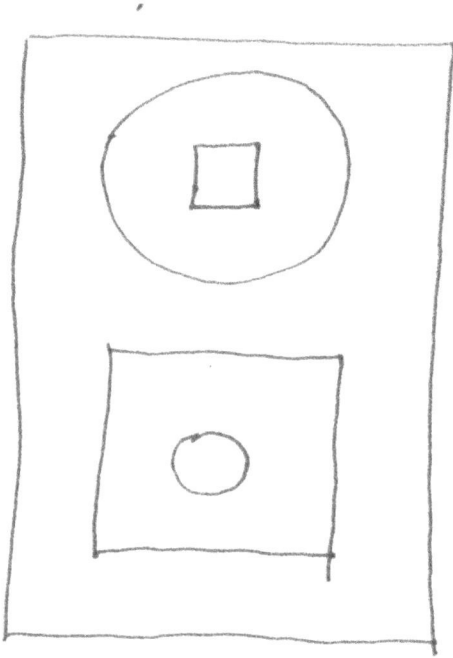

Thought can be evoked by
putting smaller, contrasting
objects within larger shapes.
Metaphysics is variation on this.

*Nathan Coppedge*

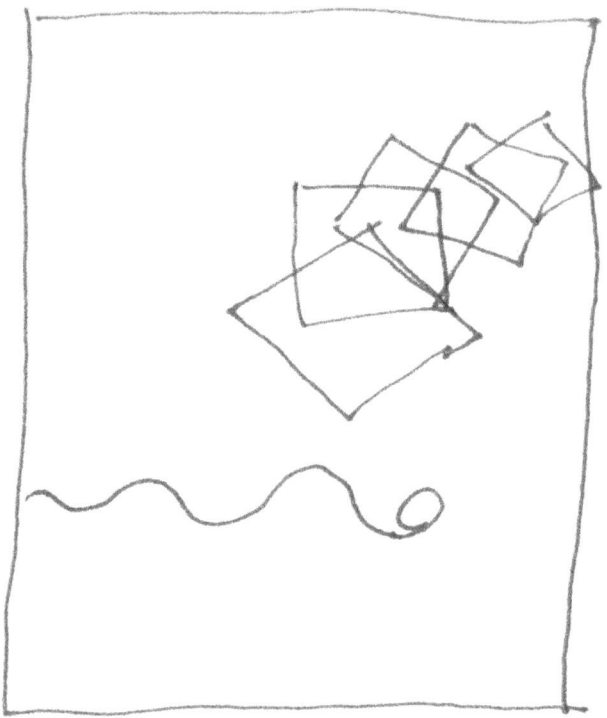

Style can be added by extending and twisting shapes.

*Nathan Coppedge*

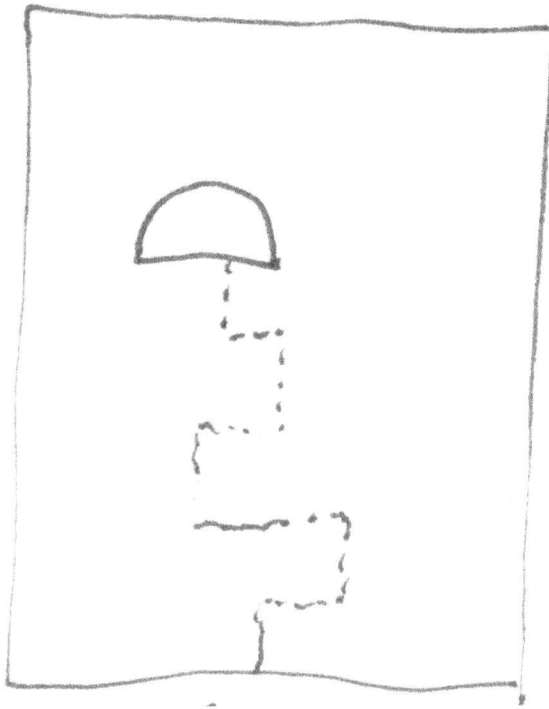

Half-shapes require half-
answers: ambiguity.

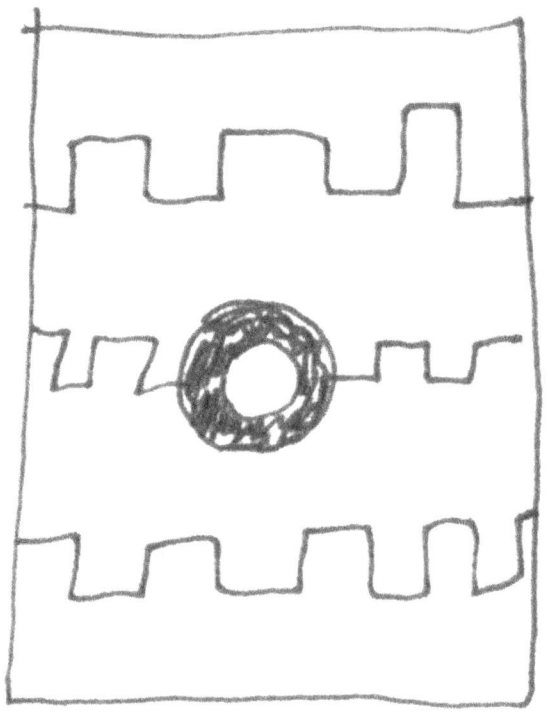

Bold shapes require a lot
of compensation.

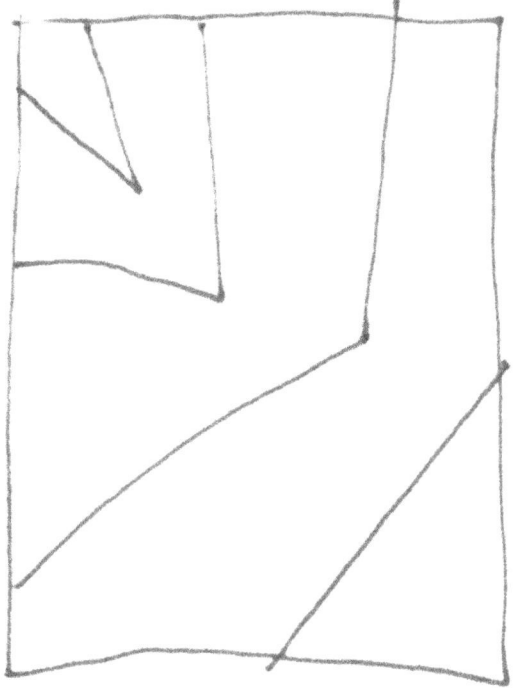

Reptition is an invitation
for variation.

*Nathan Coppedge*

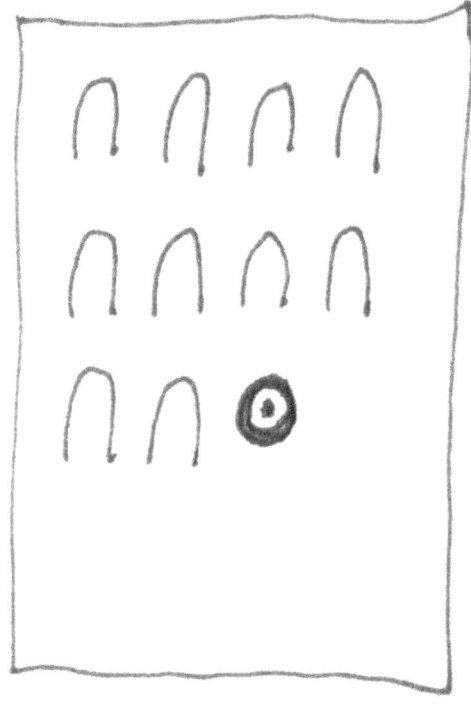

Identical forms worship
exceptions.

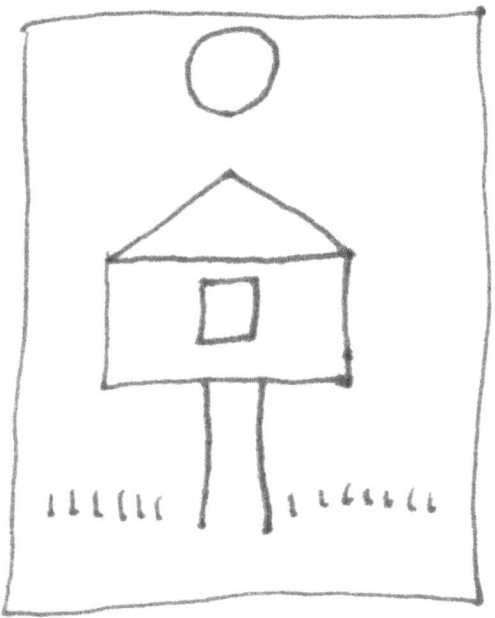

Symmetry is improved with functions.

*Nathan Coppedge*

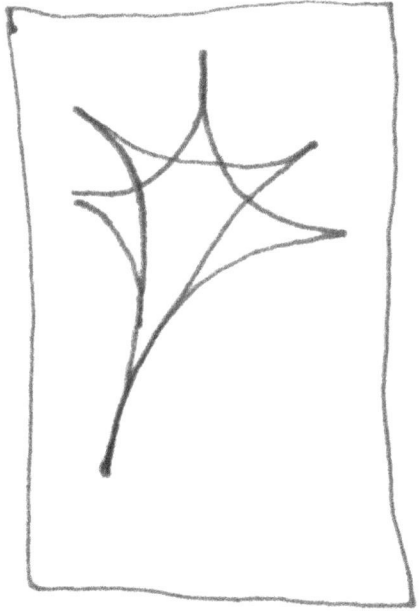

The idea is originality.

*Nathan Coppedge*

## (THE) METAPHYSICAL ART:

By Nathan Coppedge

The metaphysical art is the art of changeless variations. Here are motions within the art:

(A) There are two boulders of equal size. Place an equally-sized boulder between them.

(B) There is a small boulder and a very large boulder. Place a medium-sized boulder between them.

(C) There is a small boulder and a very large boulder. Imagine an infinite boulder beyond the large boulder.

(D) There is a small boulder and a very large boulder. Find something small and magical in the sand beyond the smaller boulder. If you do not find something, do your best to put something small and magical there in place of the missing object. If you return later, take the object, or return the object, creating a cycle of nature.

(E) Swing a cheap object on a string, to advertise the one small magical object that you do not possess, or the infinite ones that you do, but which may be invisible.

(F) Make compositions out of precious objects, finding magic in them. Think if you must.

(G) Try to balance something on a tall pole stuck in the ground. If you cannot balance the object, then become a tragedian by worshipping the invisible things on the end of the protruding stick.

(H) Pretend you are a victim to lament the possible loss of immortality. Stick sticks in the ground and lie on your back underneath the sticks, like you have been impaled by the invisible. Construct a spirit to equal the ghosts on the ends of the poles.

(I) Carry a stick to keep in touch with the ghosts in things. Become animated with the way of the world.

(J) Put a precious magical thing on a string around your neck. Now you don't need to play victim. Give it a name, like 'wishing stone' or 'philosopher's stone' or 'washing-stone' or 'stone of youth'.

(K) If you don't like the stone, throw it in the water. When you feel thoughtful, look for a replacement stone. If you love the stone, keep it on a shelf. Become a hermit.

(L) Ruminate, so that you remember just how things are.

(M) Practice un-attachment, and learn time-travel.

At this point, if you succeed, you have mastered metaphysics for three dimensions.

## ON AESTHETICS By Nathan Coppedge

One may begin in an arbitrary place with aesthetics. It involves experience. It involves the experience *of* things. In the highest sense, it is the experience of things which are immaterial. In a middle sense, it involves appreciation of context and subject, of *interactions*, of *effects*, of *problems.* In the low sense, it is an irreverence for objects which do not fulfill our desires.

There is a deception that the aesthetic sense involves an appreciation of specific objects 'just as they are'. For example, someone may think that a sculpture is a block of stone --- which is certainly true in some sense to Aristotle --- his logic being that aesthetics can be seen as a domain of logic as well. His view was one in which logic could become an art form. Things are not often so justified as they once were. But certainly aesthetics emerge. And it is with aesthetics that we have an advantage against Classicism.

Another deception is that aesthetic sense involves the appreciation of the 'properties' of objects qua property, which is not really true. A painting can be a painting even without paint, if it has the same visual effect. Artists have been discovering this over and over again. The prima facie artistic thing to do would be to arrange flowers in the shape of a

**49**

painting. But not everyone has the flowers, and so, in some sense, the flowers are a material sensibility as well. There is, in this direction, an appeal to abstraction. Abstraction is the universal within the material, as someone may have said.

What makes art ART? I argue it is a radical contingency. To some extent art is a mind-body dualism between perfection and sensibility. It cannot have one, it must have both. Yet, perfection is open to interpretation, and the point of view is not always contemporaneous with the work of art. Thus, the contingency is also a critical and historical one. One should, according to my argument, find the appropriate abstraction or the appropriate criticism, for the material of history. Yet, as it turns out, history is already abstract. Therefore, art requires a materialism of some type, but it also requires an operating idea. Art is animated by history, or materials are animated *for* history---opposite statements. What emerges from aesthetics is an idea of the object directed towards the significance of the individual, or art directed away from the artist, and collected in memory of his or her heroism. In this sense, art is interactive, or else passive and mysterious.

There is a temptation, finally, to pursue art in an ordinary sense. The temptation is a temptation for the knowable in art ---- perhaps not the predictable, but at least the understandable. And, *reductio ad absurdium*, the understandable is that which fails to make a genuine statement. Instead, it merely acquires unquestioned associations, which mark off the work as yet another example of the best and highest thing --- a case of mere examples, like skeletons in a museum. This is a way to make an impression, I argue, but it is not a way to make art. The unquestioned things may have metaphysics going for them, but they do not have style, or relevance.

Art is then a pursuit of the New, rather than the old. Things which have become mere examples, things which have been *digested*, are reference points for the current, actual definition of art. This may bring a rancor up the noses of those who feel themselves aging like a dated art object. But it does appear to secure a role for art --- as the avant-garde, the timely impression, what in my mind is not ephemera at all, but an attempt at permanent significance, an attempt at perenniality.

Immortal art is then that which is 'eternally new'. It is that which construes an original fixation upon textures, materials, ideas, histories, etc. The art of the art world is then several things: critical art, which aims to determine the new from the old, naïve art, involving the appearance of newness, theoretical art, involving concepts which could be new or old, and the avant-garde, which strives to be immortal.

In a purely symbological view, buildings and terrain can be seen as chance or chosen combinations of 'substances' ---- arcane, historical, or aesthetical ---- such as water and clay, or wood, fossilized wood, and dynamite, or concrete, silver, and milk. These kinds of 'Arcanum' provide a deeper spiritual significance that can serve to undercut and replace missing coherencies. The aesthetic becomes the ultimate phenomenal engineer, creating a falsifiable ideal, whereas the historical provides a common mode of critique between the aesthetical and the deeper, arcane realm of innate significance. Where the arcane is frangible, therefore, it becomes possible to criticize history, and introduce aesthetical forms of critique. But it is only when criticism is replaced that the aesthetical has its fullest authority.

*Nathan Coppedge*

**OTHER WORKS ON AESTHETICS
BY NATHAN COPPEDGE**

*THE HIGH ART*

*HYPER-CUBISM*

*SUBLIMISM*

*THE BOOK OF UNIQUES*

# •nathan coppedge•

Nathan Coppedge is a philosopher, artist, inventor, and poet in some capacity. He is a member of the International Honor Society for Philosophy, and has been quoted on Book Forum and the Hartford Courant. A comment at The Economist cites his possible influence on the economic policy of India. For his work on perpetual motion machines, one website puts him in the ranks of Einstein and Newton. He is also an artist in Hyper-Cubism who has produced over 1000 works. His academic articles span such subjects as objective knowledge, metaphysics, psychology, and immortality. He lives alone in New Haven, CT.